I Got a Pet!

My Pet Fish

By Brienna Rossiter

www.littlebluehousebooks.com

Copyright © 2023 by Little Blue House, Mendota Heights, MN 55120. All rights reserved. No part of this book may be reproduced or utilized in any form or by any means without written permission from the publisher.

Little Blue House is distributed by North Star Editions:
sales@northstareditions.com | 888-417-0195

Produced for Little Blue House by Red Line Editorial.

Photographs ©: Shutterstock Images, cover, 4, 6–7, 9, 10, 15, 16, 19, 21, 22–23, 24 (top left), 24 (top right), 24 (bottom left), 24 (bottom right); iStockphoto, 13

Library of Congress Control Number: 2022901949

ISBN
978-1-64619-588-6 (hardcover)
978-1-64619-615-9 (paperback)
978-1-64619-667-8 (ebook pdf)
978-1-64619-642-5 (hosted ebook)

Printed in the United States of America
Mankato, MN
082022

About the Author

Brienna Rossiter is a writer and editor who lives in Minnesota.

Table of Contents

My Pet Fish 5

Fun to Watch 11

Fish Care 17

Glossary 24

Index 24

My Pet Fish

I have pet fish.

I like to watch them swim.

My fish live in a tank.

The tank has small rocks on the bottom.

It has plants, too.

The tank has a filter.

The filter cleans the water.

Fun to Watch

The tank has glass sides.

I can see through the glass.

I watch my fish.

I do not tap on the glass.

Instead, I just look.

My fish are fun to watch. Their scales are bright colors.

Fish Care

I feed my fish.

They eat flakes of fish food.

I drop the food into their tank.

I clean my fish's tank.

First, I clean the glass.

Then, I change the water.

I use a tube to take out some water.

I add new water.

I check the tank's filter, too.

I make sure it is working well.

Glossary

filter

scales

flakes

tank

Index

C
cleaning, 8, 18

F
food, 17

G
glass, 11–12, 18

W
water, 8, 20

24